wo Rant Two Rant Two Ro

The
LOST ART
of
LOSING

Gregory Norminton

Vagabond Voices
Glasgow

© Gregory Norminton 2011

Vagabond Voices Publishing Ltd.
Glasgow
Scotland

ISBN 978-1-908251-06-0

The author's right to be identified as author of this book under
the Copyright, Designs and Patents Act 1988 has been asserted.

Printed and bound in Poland

Cover design by Mark Mechan

The publisher acknowledges subsidy towards
this publication from Creative Scotland

For further information on Vagabond Voices, see the website,
www.vagabondvoices.co.uk

To Emma

One writes not because one has something to say
but
because one has the *longing* to say something.

E.M. Cioran

Let the grass grow over it.

Georg Christoph Lichtenberg

Introduction

If there is a literary endeavour more remote from present tastes than a book of aphorisms, it has to be that book's introduction. Anything worth forking out for, in time or money, should speak for itself and not require a proleptic defence. Yet it's my contention that the aphorism – a resilient bug in the jungle of letters – has qualities to recommend it, and that its briskness ought to sit well with a culture in which just about everyone tweets, or will have twat ere long.

Other forms possess, like Claudette Colbert showing her leg in *It Happened One Night*, assets worth slowing down for: the absorption of narrative, the imprint of facts. The aphorism, exposing its slender thumb to traffic, has little to recommend it save brevity and concision. But these are qualities with cachet, too often absent from baggy novels or hackneyed journalism. Aphorisms cannot support the structure of an argument: they are fragments, yet like the shards of a mirror they reflect, they sparkle. Nor do they make excessive claims on our time. No one ever needed marooning on a desert island finally to get down to reading La Rochefoucauld. Indeed, it would take a kind of mania to read a collection of aphorisms all the way through. They may have a cumulative effect, but on the whole, they are to be sampled, not devoured in one sitting.

Your brain, to put it another way, is a cracker. And this is your dip.

I should like to claim that these aphorisms are the fruit of years of toil in the form. But reading them, who would believe it? The truth is that I am prone to sudden and shifting enthusiasms. Having enjoyed the aphorisms of Don Paterson, I followed the trail of his influences to immerse myself in E.M. Cioran (a miserabilist to give Beckett a run for his money, if only they weren't both dead), Paul Valéry, Antonio Porchia ("I know what I have given you; I do not know what you have received") and Georg Christoph Lichtenberg, whose *Waste Books* have been reissued by NYRB Classics. These writers are as different in philosophy and manner as they are removed from one another in time and geography. What they share is a gift for concision, paradox and memorable utterance.

It was perhaps inevitable that exposure should bring me out in a rash. Long possessed of strong opinions and an overdeveloped sense of engagement with issues over which I have no influence, I tried my hand at a few remarks. The few became many, and I was hooked: composing as I walked, mulling over the *mot juste*, covering scraps of paper in the attempt to chisel a hunch or grievance into a lapidary statement. The compulsion – more costive than is graphomania, but not unrelated to it – gripped me for much of a

8

year. The resulting book has no overarching purpose or polemical intent. It is made up of fragments that cohere only in as much as they come from one mind, one bundle of neuroses and preoccupations.

Much has changed in my circumstances since I wrote *The Lost Art of Losing*. I have married, found work as a university lecturer (exchanging writing time for the security of a salary) and moved with my wife from Edinburgh to Manchester. The personal happiness of these developments might seem at odds with the grim waggishness of my aphorisms. Yet the world at large has done nothing to discredit their pessimism. If anything, circumstances seem immeasurably worse than they did a year ago. The ice caps are melting, the fat cats are purring; we look for Churchills and Roosevelts and all we get is Chamberlains and Hoovers. Nor is there consolation for the author in watching his anathemas turn into prophecy. But then it doesn't take an aphorist to read the writing on the wall.

Gregory Norminton,
Manchester, December 2011

The
LOST ART
of
LOSING

Concerned for the environment, she insists on taking reusable bags whenever she flies to New York to do her shopping.

The instant S dropped the first lobster in the pot, I knew that – save for those who love me – my own death will be of no more consequence.

Death is nothing to be afraid of. Which misses the point: it is nothing that we fear.

The dominant mode of the aphorism tends to be sourness: evidence of its inadequacy as a form – if we seek in literature the sum of human experience.

Even paradox looks glib when it makes an exhibition of itself.

Admiring new hedgerows, young woods – the slow restoration of "improved" farmland – I wonder if progress and vandalism are distinguishable only with hindsight.

Should Paradise exist, our instincts would have to be filtered out of us by death, or else we'd ruin the place.

✢

Our nostalgia for the country condemns us all to the suburbs.

✢

My contract with the landscapes I value must be never to live in them.

✢

The sense of my own mediocrity descending on me like sleep.

✢

Our gaze is the tribute that beauty demands of us. The bloody tyrant.

✢

There are few things less desirable than misdirected desire.

✢

Prone to sudden enthusiasms, I leave the main work undone. The pursuit of novelty is the evasion of effort.

The truth may set you free, but it's cold outside.

For Proust, it was a madeleine. Yesterday, the smell of a particular blend of mud restored me to my childhood.

Some neuroses are companions for life. I still look under my pillow for the spider that hid there in 1983.

Truth is complex, lies are simple. Fiction confronts this challenge by wearing its untruth on its sleeve – thereby asserting kinship with its supposed opposite.

Nothing kills reading more effectively than its elevation to a virtue.

Books in a ruined world would be unreadable lies.

Eight times in a million years, human beings colonised Britain. Seven times these attempts failed; why should it be any different for us?

The Earth abides, and bides its time. I like to imagine yet that our voices will be missed.

Perhaps science fiction remains niche because of its emphasis on deep time, deep space – the dizzying perspectives of the Universe. Fiction that puts us into context is safest confined to the nerd ghetto.

And yet we are tellurian. Every trip into the stars turns our faces towards home.

Why isn't bullshit listed on the Stock Exchange?

Truth runs uphill but lies need only a flick of the heel to set them rolling. No wonder the blowhards on Fox News rarely break a sweat.

If we listed Churchill's failings in the absence of his achievements, we would remember a monster.

He who desires, but acts not, has a shot at a halfway decent marriage.

We are all bigots when our sense of self depends upon it.

It is no more abject to read a book because everyone else has done so than to avoid it for the same reason.

A maths dunce, I get an inkling of the satisfaction of a well-done sum when a sentence arranges itself unimprovably. That this happens so infrequently is one of the motivations for continuing to write.

The recurrent nightmare of a Papuan warrior finds him deep in enemy territory when his comrades suddenly vanish. The techno-grunt jangling with gadgets and acronyms suffers exactly the same terror. We are no different from our ancestors – only more encumbered.

Doubtless the play in which I must perform tonight, without having learned a single line, would in the dream of an earlier incarnation have been the rowan twig with which I confronted a sabre-toothed tiger.

Finally confessed to E that I'm writing aphorisms. We agreed that our love is strong enough to survive it.

We must practise hope, if only to defy those who would throttle it.

One may dress an animal but only humans can be naked.

The body has wits that the conscious mind lacks. Pure intellect can't dance.

The tragedy of sleep is that we cannot be awake to appreciate it.

Oh, to launch oneself at parties with the relish of a child kicking through leaves!

Thought and reason are not always aligned. One must think oneself stupid in order to avoid thinking oneself stupid.

There can be no tolerating lies that kill.

Life is made of unfinishings. Temperament concludes from this either hope or despair.

What barrier will serve against the idiot tide?

Working at home – one of those days when I look at my bed surprised not to find myself in it.

I thought I was being flippant but I found it online. The only thing missing from God the Action Figure is the prefix "In–".

Innately subversive, laughter can be turned, like a spy, against the common good. We hear this in the self-congratulation of the snigger.

Some journalists fabricate, but most insist on paraphrasing the press release that does it for them.

A terrible stink in our terrible stair. We find, smeared across the front door of our tenement and on the frozen ground before it, a load of shit: the offering, perhaps, of a suppository-fired junkie. By the end of the day no one else has cleared it away; so I set to the task, fulminating against the obscenity. But then I too am an excremental being, having evacuated, just three days ago, while in the grip of a gastric bug, great quantities of unspeakable matter – into the appropriate receptacle. Our sins are all a matter of context.

Happy endings don't exist in fiction any more than in real life. They're just mutual agreements to draw a veil over the morning after.

I like imaginary books best: the novels of Kenneth Toomey and Nathan Zuckerman, the poetry of Mary Swann and Randolph Henry Ash. Only imaginary works can be perfect. They are platonic archetypes, unstinted by the finitude of existence.

The really terrible thing is dying. Most people feel sorry for those who have died but I rather admire them – as though they had just graduated in the most taxing of subjects.

The most shameful iconoclasm is the kind that's well remunerated.

Cynicism, now the glibbest of poses, once meant a moral philosophy. We didn't need the Soviet Union to trash the dialectic of progress.

Perhaps I've another reason for confusing "entomology" with "etymology". Next to beetles, God has an inordinate fondness for words.

"Fearless" is an epithet which bigots apply to themselves. An open mind grapples constantly with dread.

In certain instances academic jargon might be termed a crypto-language. Its purpose is to keep hidden the absence of content.

Online we find too easily reflections of our prejudices. "Information technology" is really just a hall of mirrors.

Curious how many now living were Cleopatra in a former life and how few the slave who emptied her chamber-pot.

The voyage of self-discovery is not without risk. What if you reach your destination and find it's a complete dump?

When we read a novel, we contract to make ourselves dupes, hence our sense of betrayal when an author defaults on the bargain.

I ended it, and felt the unassuageable contrition of the gardener who finds two writhing halves of the one worm.

Just as we've trashed the real world, we invent a virtual one to retreat into. And the cynics doubt the ingenuity of our species!

What we understand of science is only metaphors.

Oh the irony! We achieve mass literacy and Rupert Murdoch buys all the newspapers.

That ancient English sport: liberal baiting.

The innocence that we see in children is really the absence of wounds.

Sweet analgesics! Heritage peddlers always forget about toothache.

The spirit moves with action yet action moves from the spirit. Our task is to start.

We love our partners best when we don't put ourselves overmuch in their power.

A book so bad, one was grateful for the white spaces.

Unencased by dangerous metal, the pedestrian must submit to his lowly caste. I too scowl at traffic lights and fume to overtake that lumbering obstacle. Yet where are the newspaper articles lamenting pavement rage?

One day, the messengers of the world will rise up and shoot first.

Whence this suspicion that a return to mental calm is a slumbering resubmission to the usual bromides?

With luck, we may be inoculated by experience. The only immunity against stupidity is to have contracted it at least once.

Reform demands feeling but sentimentality is reactionary. Dickens's first readers could congratulate themselves on their tender feelings for Smike even as they stepped over the child prostitute in their doorway.

Toleration should not be confused with respect. Of course you are entitled to your opinion – as am I to treat it with contempt.

And vice versa. Always, vice versa.

Even at a time of health, I dread the return of my depression as though it were a kind of lucidity. Proof that the neural groove is well and truly inscribed.

Yet sometimes the joy is almost transcendent. I look at these fragments and see a blinkered soul choosing, in the words of Jeremy Taylor, "to sit upon his little handful of thorns".

In his brilliant and terrible *Disasters of War*, Goya writes "Yo lo vi" – "I saw this". And who can doubt his sincerity? We see what our imaginations will encompass. So conditioned was Goya for the worst that he could make another's eyewitness account his own.

To deny oneself love because love cools is like refusing to heat one's home in winter because the universe is heading towards entropy.

Murder is abhorrent – of innocents especially. Yet the clumsy time-traveller would not be wholly damnable who landed his vessel on Jean Calvin's crib.

Whereof we cannot speak, thereof someone will make a wisecrack.

They were two islands – between them a minch of unbridgeable yearning.

If only we *could* appeal to enlightened self-interest. The worse things get, the more the armourers will thrive.

It is comforting sometimes to love the dead but disconcerting to fancy them.

An early death is a truncated story. Thirteen years after she took her own life, I find myself wanting to catch up with S on Facebook.

If, in sleep, the subconscious reveals our repressed longings, how come I never dream of pizza?

The sacred, because inerrant, texts are few and far between. Most of us dabble in profanity.

If fatalism could mean the calm of disinvestment – a state of utter resignation – we might be released from the daily pain of hoping.

The purest aphorisms are found, not made.

When, in the insufficiently distant future, our snouts are plunged into SimWorld and iLove and VR sex parlours, some intrepid beard will stumble with eyes aflame upon this astounding technology: the *paper codex*.

Information technology has reached the apex of its usefulness: from here on it's enslavement all the way. Beware of geeks bearing gifts.

In the lost forest of Caledon, I looked up to watch a raven perform its victory spin. Such gratuitous virtuosity! It was raven celebrating raven – as life asserts its meaning in *being*.

Some birds beat the air as if it were a foe meaning to drag them down. Others seem only to flap their wings in order to keep us from getting suspicious.

Il s'est donné la mort: "he gave himself death". What does it say about a culture that it can come up with such a felicitous locution?

For years I cancelled myself out, fearing that the slightest manifestation of erotic interest would prove an imposition.

If consciousness is defined by the senses, painlessness is a kind of sleep. The instant my neuralgia hit, I was most horribly awake in it. I wanted to beat myself insensible to get away from that monstrous lucidity.

Though I look into your eyes, I cannot see what you see.

We are in love with our burrow, though it may become our tomb.

A child's tantrum is infuriating because we cannot join in.

We ought to worship, or placate, the gods of contingency. Was it Blucher who saved Wellington or a Corsican's stomach trouble?

Too much of our literature is logophagous – consuming itself, then gnawing at new growths – while the feast of the world goes unsampled beyond.

A magazine asks me to contribute regular updates on the progress of my writing. Though flattered, I take against the idea. It would be like publicising the weekly condition of my sputum.

Our ingenuity far outstrips the wisdom we need to cope with its consequences.

A better word for triumph is reprieve.

Fragile at noon, I tell myself: never again. "Yeah, right," says my liver – the most sarcastic of vital organs.

Perhaps thunder is the sound of God slapping His forehead in pure disbelief.

Men assert, women know.

A great artist, for a time, will be a conduit for a voice scarcely her own. Something utters through this mortal – who is bereft, used up, when the voice departs. Talent may remain, while gusts of the former gift will rise up from the lungs, but devoted fans are hanging about an empty vessel, wondering when it will astound them again.

The fox and the hedgehog have their domains, but what beast represents the rest of us, who know nothing save our opinions?

The poetic response to Schrödinger's thought experiment is to ask: what colour is the cat?

For fear of being axiomatic, we prefer our aphorisms to sparkle than to be true.

When the sun is at its height, our shadows, out of shame, cower between our feet.

Thwarted pleasures stimulate our imagination in order for us to partake of what we missed. We regret things undone in the past in order to enrich our present.

Literature will always be a shadow of the world. The best-wrought poem is an object less worthy of our admiration than the hand which wrote it.

When success eludes us, we learn to take comfort from the consistency of our failures.

Aliens came to Earth and sought at once a meeting with its most successful species. They are still waiting for the cockroaches to speak.

A bestselling author complains of pressure to keep churning out variations on the *same book*. I, on the other hand, can write whatever I please. The fear of being pigeonholed is one of the perquisites of success.

After a morning at my computer, I end with fewer words than when I started: reassuring proof that I am getting somewhere.

Even on his off-days he could not disappoint, and people would have commented with satisfaction on the remarkable absence of an aphorism from Dr Johnson.

No dream of loved and lost relations has haunted me more deeply than the magical second kittenhood of my dead cat last night.

Bring on the firestorms, the floods and megadroughts – if only to wipe the smirk off their faces.

Poetry names the darkness, lighting nothing. And yes, I intend that ambiguity.

M's high standards, his reticence to publish all save the best, the most durable of his writing, makes me feel like a flasher who braves the streets offering a magnifying glass to his victims.

Of course newborns look ancient: they've just come in from eternity.

The male academic waggles his few but impressive facts, as a caterpillar, soft and edible, raises its forked appendage to give the impression that a snake is at the other end of it.

Testosterone can make a competition out of anything. Somewhere, probably, there's a birdwatching club whose first rule is that it mustn't be spoken of.

Unequal to the task of changing our ways, we put our hopes in a techno-fix as we would hide in mummy's skirts. But we have no mummy. We are orphans.

Those who defend God are really defending themselves.

Our last illusions about the solidity of the world vanish when we become parents and realise that the ground we stand on is ourselves.

The more conscious I become of my impotence, the more I behave as if the world would collapse if I didn't keep an eye on it. And I wonder how crackpots come into being...

Could the older generation's aversion to climate science be rooted in fear of its proximal death? If so, it is a declaration of war against the future they don't have: the monstrous solipsism of ensuring that they take everyone with them.

What's blindingly obvious cannot be looked at.

I will never cease wishing for his death – even if it takes me his lifetime to succeed.

We declare the person fascinating who listens to us longest.

The path to success runs through other people's vanity.

Sometimes a typo gets to the heart of things. Just found on a green issues blog: "Grab your coast, apocalypse watchers".

There are Hamlets who, deprived of a ghost, become Polonius: their art gone to seed for want of matter.

Fearing I'll outstay my welcome presupposes that I began with one.

One cannot admire the nerve of a nerveless person.

If we could reconcile ourselves, truly, to the fact that no one's watching, what fun we might get up to.

How glibly, in our disputes, we equate ourselves with people from the past. Only time will tell who is Galileo and who the Inquisition.

The sceptic's burden is always lighter.

I resent sharing my apple with a maggot, but how must the maggot feel to find my teeth in its dining-room?

Politics may require a fudge but the biosphere doesn't do compromises. Even if you leap three-quarters of the way, you still end up in the ditch.

This bold hypothesis has been doing the rounds in learned journals for years now. The academic is the school swot who does the journalist's work for him.

The *grand-père terrible* of English fiction publishes a new novel. "Hardly anyone reads him," a journo quips. The word "him" in the phrase is redundant.

Who can evaluate utility? There are plenty of things one can live without that give one a reason for living.

Even as we read we forget, and what remains to us is not essence but residuum.

Sometimes a word does double duty, both conveying and embodying its meaning. How appropriate, for instance, that English has no exact translation for *recherché*.

Setting aside the biological impossibility, we could not exist *intellectually* without the natural world. All our referents are there: take away the sea of troubles, the tangled web, the roots and ramifications, and we could only stammer, idiots in our spaceship.

Send in the drones, engage the robot soldiers, and our enemies will intensify their attacks on civilians. Flesh will answer for flesh: let the pilots at their computer consoles remember that.

It would take an eternity to work our way back to the first wrong turning.

We cherish babies because we see our future in them; we shun the elderly for the same reason.

Conceived on the go, dragged in haste towards its consignment, the aphorism slipped clear of my mind and attained perfection.

Read glancingly, these fragments settle on the mind like snowflakes on a warm pavement. Whether they have any cling depends on the mental space afforded them. But writers cannot control the attention of their readers: we should count ourselves lucky to have flagged one down, even if it's only to gaze forlornly at the receding taillights.

To fear the ill-opinion of others is grossly to overestimate the space we take up in their imagination.

We can only hope by way of contrast that once in a while good comes from our acting with the worst intentions.

A nag is someone who pursues us with the truth.

One cold winter here (though freakishly warm elsewhere) and the public loses its belief in global warming. We cannot distinguish between weather and climate, just as we cannot distinguish between ourselves and the world.

Why is there something rather than nothing? Because nothing could not ask itself that question.

A visited city lacks the ley lines of habit. The tourist and I do not walk down the same street.

When I talk to myself, do I imagine that someone else is listening?

After a time that might have been an afternoon and might have been a century, Lucifer ordered his minions to take down the sign. "All hope abandon ye who enter here" was an instruction that deprived Hell of its most effective torture.

In the psychopathic conduct of the Olympian gods, antiquity prepared the mind for Stalin.

To the cold, stony edifice I mean to add my little heap of pebbles.

This happened, then this, and then this. Now spare yourself the trouble of reading that bestseller.

The trick of obscurity is vital to things that perish in daylight.

The kites that he feeds each morning would just as happily peck at his corpse. Now here's the twist: that knowledge consoles him.

The sometime pleasure of a second glance. What I took, with an inner grumble, for litter becomes a hillside of snowdrops.

Oh yes, I'm an eco-hypocrite. I deplore consumerist greed and the lack of it among book buyers.

With the fall of the press and the rise of the blog, the age of the hack is passing into history. Now, *pace* Johnson: No man but a blockhead ever wrote, except for pleasure.

The devil may have all the best tunes but God has some memorable chords.

The tragedy for conservatives is that everything changes; for progressives, that it does so in the wrong direction.

What they failed to strangle in the crib they smother in its dotage.

I need a thesaurus of *ideas*.

Poetry has its limitations. I may call that clot of phlegm a liquid lichen but you will still step around it.

We stoop to pick up our dogs' turds – and we think *we* own *them*.

The seas are acidifying faster than at any time in 55 million years. We read this and move on. For all our computers, we cannot compute.

Animals have no name for our species yet they know to avoid it.

We call vermin anything that exploits us.

If a truth falls on deaf ears, does it make a sound?

Of all my poses, the prophet of doom is the one she least wants to marry.

Love has one language but many dialects.

Haggard, I shut my door on the lot of them, only to find them lolling on my sofa.

A question mark is an exclamation mark that stoops to inspect itself.

A baby is introduced not to daisies but to *the* daisy. Our first of everything is everything.

The tawdry relief when a beautiful woman opens her mouth and speaks horribly.

The soil of thought is temperament.

Parents take their kids to marvel at the reassembled T-Rex, the bones of a giant sloth. But I have seen tigers, leatherback turtles, Irrawaddy dolphins: beasts that will soon be no less extinct. Perhaps this makes my brain a museum piece.

If the internet had existed in Weimar Germany, the Nazis might never have taken power, as their thugs would have been too busy beating up their opponents online.

With the e-book, reading is reduced to a single artefact through which the text passes like a spirit through a medium. Thus the book loses its corporeal existence and literature enters the age of ghosts.

A deity worthy of worship is the product of civilisation. If things turn sour for the whole clanjamfrie, expect a return to propitiation.

Credit... Climate... Oil... It's the Imagination Crunch that frightens me.

An anthology of true (that is, unpremeditated or unembellished) last words would be a jumble of groans, platitudes and obscenities. It would chart the point at which we can no longer redeem ourselves, death being the last step on the *escalier de l'esprit*.

To the mind, our organs are resident aliens: autonomous to our will, their workings mysterious, their presence confirmed only when they crash.

If God is Truth, Satan was the first storyteller.

A novelist must look closely for her characters merely to look.

If the conceit is true, that the most vocal homophobes are shouting down their hidden natures, what does it say about me that I so readily declare other people morons?

Because we want our joys to be particular, we generalise from our disappointments.

Suffering gives an outline to the ease we failed to notice.

With its anchorites and flagellants, the Middle Ages found a use for anorexics and self-harmers, and perhaps we would have fewer of either, had not the old Church mistaken sickness for saintliness... On the other hand, pain will always be with us, and perhaps we have merely swapped meaning for morphine.

"Sustaining illusion" in *Nostromo*: the revelatory word in Conrad's formulation is not the second but the first. Let Tolkien freaks raise their kids in Elvish if it makes them happy and kind.

The randomness of suffering being intolerable, humanity invented malediction.

When we object to science's attempt to dethrone us – to place human beings in the commonwealth of species – we would do well to recall the fate of most tyrants.

You know you have to write when you seriously imagine that having a bibliography will lessen the anguish of your deathbed.

Our aim must be for life to flourish in our wake.

The gap between revelation and platitude is time.

Another day, another prospect to squander.

I read that Michel Leiris, in a book called *Manhood*, compared writing to bullfighting, for the courage required of the participants. This is priceless. The only thing in common between the torero and the writer is the word "bull".

Don't be too hard on yourself. There's a whole universe for that.

I have a head for books and factoids, with too little space left over for life. E, on the other hand, remembers everything. She contemplates in retrospect a furrowed field, while I look back upon trees in fog.

The aphorist must peep through cracks. To see things whole would shame us into silence.

We are humble in the hope of being praised for our humility.

I took fewer drugs than my friends, having fewer brain cells to spare.

If at first you don't succeed, get a man in.

Do politicians speak like politicians at home?
"My policy of fidelity towards you, my darling, is
aspirational rather than a target..."

With its fusion of intimacy and anonymity,
immediacy and inconsequence, the internet is a pool
for our lowest instincts to paddle in. As for online
politics forums, they expose the id at the start of
ideology.

We traduce the world when we fail to wonder at it.

Don't sweat about the flames, the flood will put
them out.

He can't love; she can't empathise. There can be no
legislating for hidden disabilities.

According to Swift, Man is *rationis capax*: a species capable of reason. We are also capable of running 100 metres in under ten seconds, but it's not a talent given to many.

As we grow older we slow down because we can glimpse our destination.

It doesn't take much – a couple of tramps relieving themselves in our tenement stair – to turn me from liberal Quaker to fascist eugenicist. What would I become if *sorely* tested?

The failure of extraterrestrial intelligence to contact us may well be proof of its existence.

At the root of our inaction is a refusal to credit the normalisation of catastrophe. Where is it written that reality cannot be outlandish?

Of all own goals, few are as humiliating as having our self-deprecation taken literally.

The bright blessed day – except for insomniacs.

People's faces when they read. I like especially those who look quietly *indignant*.

Sometimes, throwing a book across the room is the only possible form of criticism.

Be wary of polemic. A novel lands heavily when launched from a pulpit.

Under the greed for all there is to read, a colder current runs: when will the output cease?

The writer's task: to search hard for something that looks found.

When the last forests vanish, so will the words for describing what we have lost.

A published writer is like an archer who cannot find his arrows. Who knows if any found its target?

If the words find you in a rainstorm, get wet for them.

The peculiar melancholy of leafing through a decades-old literary journal. All that hope and promise that never came to fruition, or did so unregarded, while history slobbered on.

A hundred percent cure for my bibliophilia: boycott all book outlets that stock nothing of mine.

Don't reconcile yourself to disappointment: make a home in it.

I don't believe in ghosts, fear seeing one, and resent their failure to reveal themselves to me.

Every phase of our lives is passing; we are only uniquely present the moment we cease – whereupon we are gone.

Don't imagine that you can say anything new. Hope at best for some felicitous rephrasing.

Power does not need censorship. It has only to co-opt the human desire not to know.

Amnesia can be bought and forgetfulness hastened by such interests as are inconvenienced by remembrance. Regarding America, and with apologies to Lichtenberg: Let the Astroturf be laid over it.

Make it specific. The word to avoid in descriptive prose is "some".

We can only maintain promise by not attempting to realise it. Even then, the damp rises.

Lovers who have tongues for each other but eyes only for the street display in public not affection but a conjoined narcissism.

The past is a work in progress.

Reading bad writing can be instructive but it leaves a bad vibe in the brain that corrupts the good writing we read to recover from it. A degraded public discourse taints thought in much the same way. How can we breathe freely when the air is thick with cliché?

Know that you're a fool, but don't treat yourself like one.

Publishing is an industry – with all that implies of tenderness towards its raw materials.

Children don't really believe in bogeymen. Governments do.

An aphorism disdains a proverb to console itself for its own obscurity.

Everyone seems to have a second home who lives in Dumfries and Galloway.

Certain lessons cannot be taught, only learned.

Your writing must reach beyond you – otherwise publication is a grotesque attempt to impose yourself on others.

Is suicide uniquely human? I have watched ducks attempt to drown themselves countless times, yet they always bottle it at the last moment.

"He has paid his debt to nature"; how astute the phrase. Yet we have lived so long on credit that our deaths will scarcely pay off the interest.

Descriptive realism risks a Pooterish accumulation. Sterne and Diderot were free to play; later novelists were constrained by the furniture. And yet too precise a narrative – containing an exact sufficiency of detail and only such dialogue as illuminates character or advances the plot – will smell of artifice because not one word is superfluous. Life is full of waste and redundancy. It needs the ordering that art can give, but if life's imitation is too tightly choreographed, all we notice is the dancers and not the dance.

Eventually, given its mania for conspiracy theories, the radical right will accuse the polluting industries of a scam to keep environmentalists in work.

Even the best writers have their faults, and the race for universal acclaim cannot be won. Endeavour then to fail as interestingly as possible.

My one instance of seeming emulation has been to plagiarise a famous author *pre-emptively*. Though you write first, you cannot publish second.

I don't need to make it big, only to make it through.

Mangled they may be, and public transport for fleas, yet we should value pigeons. I can't imagine anyone from the Council eating vomit off our doorsteps on a Sunday morning.

Beware the unreluctant prophet of doom.

My agent sends me my Life Sales figures. She might as well have posted a package containing a sharp-edged sheet of paper and a slice of lemon.

Small *r* relativism offers only limited protection against unpleasant realities. If I am stamping on your head, that's a fact, not a point of view.

When Americans meet a billionaire, they wonder how he did it. When Europeans meet the same, we wonder who he did it to.

Mid-June, yet on the mountains thin eyelets of snow remain. Admiring those pristine patches, I dream of making the ascent and despoiling them with my boot prints.

There was a time when I'd have thought I could wing it. Now I'm confident only of getting into a flap.

The ghost orchid has become extinct. In dying out it lived up to its name.

Become extinct? Language can encompass non-existence only through its opposite. Similarly, "he is dead" is a kind of evasion. Even the pronoun is of questionable validity.

A heartbeat for some is the rhythm of life, for others a countdown.

F's assertion, all those years ago, that he would pray for me, remains in my memory unsurpassed as an act of verbal aggression.

Most of us fear extinction. Beckett feared that he might not achieve it.

I take my sister's Labrador for a walk, and suddenly reticent Hampshire might be rural Ireland. The English own dogs in order to talk to one another.

In private, the prude longs to shed a letter.

Consented, perhaps, even married, but no one ever *fancied* out of pity.

A paddling pool of a man, the shallows of B's personality sufficed to drown his children.

A stroke of luck is a blow to addicts of complaint.

Man is the cherub with a forked tail.

You wouldn't take a dump in front of a friend, yet we do in front of the mirror, which is our enemy.

Checking out a girl on the train when she scratches back a sleeve to reveal a forearm hatched with scars, each one a spectral laceration on my prying eyes.

There is privilege inherent in complaint; the powerless know that no one is listening.

Incessantly we ask the meaning of life to protect us from hearing the perfectly obvious answer.

Genetic determinism overlooks the possibility that we are hardwired to *transcend* our natures.

As if to prove how far we've fallen, the encomia on the back of a book on kindness declare it a "call to arms" and "a little hand-grenade of a book".

How many in church on Sunday pray not to God, but for God to exist?

Past thirty, all exercise is mere postponement.

That summer, the mosquito, conscience, kept me awake.

Virtue belongs to those who resist a harmful talent. You cannot admire the honesty of a lousy liar.

Perfect memory would paralyse a writer, as we would know each time we trod on someone else's sentences.

Some things must be seen through to be seen.

To hate someone is to assume a kind of intimacy with them; hence the electorate's rage against politicians, fomented because the object of hatred cannot return it.

We all know the punishment of Tantalus, yet is there a mythical torment based on *indecision*?

Effort can only get you so far. Consider the four-foot tennis ace, the six-foot jockey: one cannot grow nor the other shrink into the fulfilment of their gifts.

It is because we look for patterns that we find them, though they need not be proof of a design. Precognition is merely the coincidence we've remembered.

Both assaults came as painful shocks to me, yet it should have been obvious that a lout isn't going to change suddenly for the better when you define him to his face.

The shallowest minds go off the deep end.

A play of excruciating mediocrity wins plaudits in Edinburgh, on account, perhaps, of the painful experiences that inspired it. And sure, the absence of sincerity will tarnish a work, yet its presence in abundance is no substitute for art.

It takes a strong stomach to have a clear eye.

Sometimes you feel doubly awake, for a minute only, or a few seconds, and the world is charged with grandeur. Perhaps we need the pettiness of our preoccupations in order to keep our heads from exploding.

Might the hidden grounds of religious opposition to masturbation be that it is a form of incest?

Even in the deserts we are all on thin ice.

Why do political journalists associate smiling with a "human face"? A scowl, a grimace, a sneer are no less representative of the species.

Popular hostility to the knowledge that we are animals baffles me, as therein lies our only hope of absolution.

If a virus could think as we do, it too would imagine itself to be exceptional.

Some couples separate to escape the loneliness of being together.

The left patronises in word, the right in deed. This may be why so many working-class Americans vote Republican. We prefer to be exploited for our ignorance than to be informed of it.

The greatest danger for aphorists is that they affect the smugness of the disabused. No one is more readily duped than a smartarse.

It is always a surprise to us that other people behave exactly as we do.

To withstand your grief, offer it as tribute to the one extinct.

Even without the accent, I betray my Englishness by complaining about the weather. To a Glaswegian, rain is just another word for air.

If all hated peoples around the world obeyed the command to "go back where they came from", there would be some serious overcrowding in the Great Rift Valley.

One of the crueller ironies of the ecological crisis is that our noblest instincts are subverted. The impulses to breed, to feed and hoard for the security of our young, have all become deadly urges, while the sterility of the miser is a gesture of solidarity with the future.

With European flights grounded, gone was the need to leap on a plane to escape the din of aircraft.

Sexual propriety is the want of opportunity promoted to a virtue.

Stare long enough at your reflection and you will see, with a creak of panic, not your own features but those, utterly strange, of your fellow man.

Thanks to modern communications, we can watch a catastrophe unfold, in real time, on the far side of the world. Technology makes us hobbled gods, all-seeing yet powerless to intervene.

When, in old age, her last lover died, she declared herself a virgin: untouched by a living hand.

I am an evangelist for therapy. You cannot walk away from something that keeps tripping you up.

We call the Nations a Family – and then wonder why they squabble.

A tree, though rooted, is still travelling.

Behind every aphoristic assertion there should be the watermark of a question.

Another job application comes to naught. What I call, self-consolingly, fate is really just a lack of qualifications.

If a man treads on your toe, tread on his, but first remove your foot from under it.

It's easy to be cocksure in expecting the worst. Nobody defines themselves as cautiously pessimistic.

Truth is the goal but plausibility is the destination.

Our chickens coming home to roost have the hunch and lope of vultures.

It would be easier to pin our hopes on humanity if we did not belong to it. Knowing myself, I have few illusions.

Whence this cultural hostility to childlessness, whereby those who have chosen to resist the selfish gene find themselves accused of egotism?

In defence of the aphorism, we can at least agree that of all forms it is the most useless for those wishing to ingratiate themselves with the reader.

Reading Marcus Aurelius on the loo, it occurs to me that wisdom is neither progressive nor cumulative. It must be reiterated. This need not be a cause for gloom: it means that the dead can always surprise us.

Constancy in politics is pitched as a virtue, and yet to change our mind is to demonstrate that we still have one.

Perhaps we weep because our weeping alters nothing.

Good prose takes the long way round in pursuit of a short cut to the reader.

Where we cannot bring change, let us at least irk.

Only when we suffer personally are we roused to evasive action. For most of us, a tarred gannet is no reason to cycle after an oil spill.

Many that boast about their love of liberty overstate their commitment. I'm all for free speech but I suspect the only thing that I would defend to the death is my life.

The concept of entropy is bodied forth in language: what once blazed with significance is now cold and dull in our mouths.

If clichés travelled as light does, somewhere in the galaxy it would be possible to look on them as they shone formerly, with the dazzle of revelation.

We search in vain for life among the stars, and do not know what our shit encounters when it hits the bottom of the ocean.

Banter: what oft was thought but ne'er deemed worth expressing.

The sexual allure of the cinema rests on a partial overwhelming of the senses. If the smell of a movie star were amplified in proportion to the image, we would settle more happily for our sublunary lovers.

In idleness the meanest tasks grow monstrous and we fly to work to escape the burdens of leisure.

The foam, the roar, the churn of sprinting water. Sitting on this rocky ledge, staring into the white rush, my ears clogged with it: like a dream of water, in which I am fully awake.

He got away with his crime. The luck of it pursued him as relentlessly as any Fury.

Perhaps only negative perfection is possible. The most luminous success cannot boast the integrity of complete failure.

At least he had the decency to hate himself: is there a hypocrite to match a self-approving misanthrope?

There are abysses into which we are not permitted not to look – if only for the length of time it takes to fall down them.

"Who could have foreseen [enter the latest fuck-up]. " How many falls, how many slumps and crashes, before we accept that gravity applies to all our systems?

Whatever bears up to frequent repetition is probably worth repeating.

We cannot prepare ourselves for our own ends. Even the gravedigger is a novice in death.

No wonder so many writers drink: day after day at the page, decanting one book into another...

As austerity bites, it will be the middle classes that riot. For your expectations to be dashed, you need first to have had some.

Miserabilists should be silent. Too many that profess their contempt for the world do so in hope of its admiration.

It makes sense that we should kick a man when he's down. When he's standing we might do ourselves an injury.

Powerless against those that tread on us, we stamp our feet on those below. What trickles down of wealth is not money but grievance.

The illusions that we entertain will not reciprocate.

Midterms in America – and voters, furious at their physician's ineffective treatment, raid the medicine cabinet for the bottle that poisoned them.

Larkin's "desire of oblivion" runs deep: perhaps every city aspires to become its own ruins.

Unlike writers, a field does not grow anxious while it lies fallow.

Birdsong rebuilt what sleep dismantled. Asserting his territory, the thrush showed me mine.

Life, that has no reason for being, cannot get enough of itself, and it is human pride that refuses to call this delight.

We can be motivated to save as little as a field, but no one is moved to action over a mountain of data.

Views can be blinkers. Knowing what we think, we may fail to think through what we know.

As things stand, hoping for the Earth is like asking for the moon.

Cornucopians dream perpetual abundance; deep ecologists predict apocalypse. Both are mistaken. There will be no end, only painful presents.

Perhaps death is no more than waking up in the element whence we came.

Don't ask, lest you be told and lose your appetite.

How I dread unpleasantness: I get toothache at the very thought of the bullet I must bite.

In my grandmother's edition of La Bruyère, I find her student marginalia and the redolence of a lost apartment. The electronic book is all very well; yet I doubt many readers will shed a tear over the smell of an old one.

73

There are philosophers who devote their talents to ignoring what is needful. In this regard, the world has long been governed by philosopher-kings.

We look to power to remedy error, but error is power's currency of action. All it can do is manufacture new errors under which to conceal the old.

Reality is merely the impossibility in which the world has chosen to invest.

No matter how often we smile at our reflections, we will never win over the mirror.

War, that does not work, never ceases to function. One might almost marvel at its tireless operation, until one considers the insatiability of the cancer cell.

You won't catch him grinning for his photograph. He knows how it plans to pain him, in the fullness of time.

Never apologise. Never explain. Because you're a sociopath.

✛

From rice to rye, wheat to corn, and all meat reared on the same, we are in essence herbivores. Let us pursue our holocausts of grass: patiently, implacably, it will grow over us.

✛

When proscribed virtual realities emerge, new cartels will form that look on narcotics with contempt. Technology doesn't solve problems, merely displaces them.

✛

Happiness writes white – but white refracted reveals all the colours in the rainbow.

✛

The dream of Armageddon is rooted in narcissism. A modest man feels no need to drag the world into his grave.

✛

There are no full stops in nature.

Radicalism has the security of one constant: the status quo is always unacceptable.

The truth will out. Our work in the meantime is to ensure that, when it does, it hurts as little as possible.

An aphorism is a remark that has won itself some elbow room.

Innocence cannot mean immunity. The sins of the father will cease to be inherited when the same is true of the sorrows.

Giving up meat is one step we can take towards a bloodless existence, but how much harder it is to extricate ourselves from systems that make us all cannibals by degrees.

There are forms of absorption that are outwardly focused. The novel-gazing of writers, for instance…

From a field of sheep I conclude: it's not that
animals can't stare down humans, it's that only
humans have anything to prove by the experiment.

The joy of environmentalism: in its victories even
the defeated have won. For the sorrow, read above
and substitute three antonyms.

We need the dark in the cinema, in the theatre, for
when we watch ourselves watching we cannot see.

Time does not heal all wounds. It just closes up the
scar tissue.

Blundering, this birdwatcher can empty a wood. The
beasts of the world know us better than we know
them.

As we cling to our belongings, we lose our sense of
belonging and commerce pitches *more* belongings
as the solution. The divide between salesman and
pusher is mostly statutory.

They say time gives us the face that we deserve; so does the plastic surgeon.

Word and world do not coincide. Perhaps the lion through its mighty yawn recalls Adam's attempt to name it.

For instance, in 2010, while Pakistan drowns and Russia burns, we will invest ten times more in fossil fuels than in renewables. When future generations ask what we were thinking, they will be paying us an unmerited compliment.

It seems possible that the founding question of religion is not "does god exist". Perhaps our ancestors invented god so that, believing itself to be observed, humanity might be sure of its *own* existence.

"The love of liberty," wrote Hazlitt, "is the love of others." There's another writer you won't find on a libertarian's bookshelf.

The blog is truly egalitarian, offering us all a share in the loneliness of lacking readers.

Literature is that which survives its exegetes.

We are all dying. The trick is to do it as slowly as possible.

My right ear, which cannot make out a dear friend in the pub, won't spare me the mutterings of my neighbour in the library. Similarly, though I walk past the fragrance from a rosebush, the smallest crust of dogshit on my shoe reeks to me from a room away. When you're this tuned to the negative, any positive thinking deserves a standing ovation.

Science, for all its advances, will never provide us with virtual water.

My wife wants me to acknowledge my sources. That would solve the problem of bulking out my books.

The specific dissolves the general. Labels are best left on bananas.

Too good a talker to be a writer, he burned up every impulse towards the page.

Lest they confuse the plain with the simple, campaigners for plain English should consider the words: "Is not".

What if arcadia is a place, not of refuge, but of protest?

For a century, Prometheus raged against the eagle. Gradually his suffering evolved, and that ravening beak, those piercing talons, became his reason for being, the reminder of his disobedience. At the summit of a thousand years, the eagle's visits had become his due; for only when it tore into his liver was Prometheus restored to his sun-addled self. The gods, when they came to unchain him, intended it not as liberation but as the ultimate refinement of their retribution.

The masochist can come to love most pains except himself.

Concision is a virtue only in part. The aphorism, in its brevity, also shrugs off the burden of proof.

I would prefer not to show my work in progress. Some novels, like mushrooms, grow best in the dark.

Ecological alert from the oceans! Our plastic is seriously contaminated with seawater.

Arrian recounts that Alexander the Great endured the rebuke of an Indian philosopher. "You roam presumptuously over the world, giving no rest to yourself or others. Yet soon you will die, and possess no more of the earth than suffices for your burial." Alexander praised his critic, accepted the reproof of a conquered people – then resumed his conquests. There is no truth that can be spoken to power that power cannot cheerfully ignore.

John Clare suffered two enclosures: first in fences, then in fashion.

Or let there be another version. The gods did
not punish Prometheus but made him watch as,
down the ages, humans set the world alight; until,
standing in the ashes of his hopes for mortals,
Prometheus fledged an eagle and begged the gods to
chain him to his rock.

What motivates a vandal? Envy and spite, but also
perhaps the maddening persistence of objects – the
idiot avenging himself on the world for its readiness
to outlast him.

No revelation sparkles brighter than the one
scribbled down from sleep, nor looks duller when
revisited by the light of day. What we dream is the
image of meaning. The object eludes us.

In all of us lurks the genius who knows exactly what
we mean... if only we had the means to understand
him.

Our hopes may be raised for us, but only we can lift
our heads above the parapet.

America will get there in the end – but by the end we'll be finished.

The worst have their passionate intensity and the struggle is not between faith and unbelief but between moderation and extremism.

Our ultimate regret – that everything passes – may also prove our last consolation.

That rattling at your door is the zombie, ambition, refusing to grant you the peace of its grave.

You wouldn't presume to take up an hour of a stranger's life with stories from your own; so what's with expecting two whole weeks for one of your fictions?

Just read "sales assistant" as "slaves assistant" – though which of us is meant I can't be sure.

Happiness is a by-product. Make it your goal and you will always shoot wide.

Those who deny the existence of ghosts must forget their dreams the moment they waken.

It is easier to feel guilty than to change. So long as we sprinkle it with remorse, surely we can have our sin cake and eat it?

Waited an hour for the bus and nothing came along but this poxy sentence.

Sun leaf and birdsong: a soft day with no need for hope, for life seems already to have delivered.

With his cold eye, hard nose and sharp elbows, he is the model citizen of his gated community.

We can all change for the better, but loss is the stronger current.

Ovid's *Metamorphoses*: should we prefer transformation into an olive tree or a nightingale to the shape-shifting that age has in store for us?

Good prose is like a windowpane, wrote Orwell, which may be why reading the newspaper so often feels like slashing our wrists on broken glass.

All morning tidying my life into little drawers. One day I will be tidied into a little drawer of my own.

Oh! for a time machine to fetch Thomas Paine – that he might confound those who invoke him in defence of their inanities.

Stand well back from the man who thinks he is not comic.

Familiarity can also breed comfort. Finding myself alone for the evening, I curl up with a cup of tea in front of *The Shining*.

Time is despotic. Visiting my grandmother in the geriatric ward, I felt like a Red Cross inspector in the gulag of old age.

There is vanity in self-reproach: why should *you* be immune to human failure?

The path from youthful Trot to rightwing hack is well trodden. What does not change about the mind is its *set*.

Talk about overkill. Given what we know about human beings and reality, climate change denial has spent a billion petrodollars pushing at an open door.

Home and unhelmed, I drink to drop my heart from my mouth. Anyone who doubts that might is still right has only to negotiate British roads on a bicycle.

Planning ahead, the best we can do is to choose with care our future regrets.

We treat the natural world as a mine of commodities when it is something infinitely more valuable – our deepest well of metaphor.

We have no need to hypothesise parallel universes. The world contains seven billion minds – and that's counting only the humans.

We long to capture a likeness; pin down an image; nail a phrase. It's a wonder Nabokov is the only lepidopterist in literature.

"Fair-weather friend"; there's a phrase that will make little sense to future generations.

We hate ourselves as if it were a virtue. I know people who treat their neighbour infinitely more kindly than they treat themselves.

In a sense, my rarely updated blog gives an accurate impression of my existence. Daily it publicises the failure of my good intentions.

We know from experience that we get from giving; yet we fear to call bullshit on capitalism's reversal of the formula.

Is it simplicity when it's freely chosen? Hauling logs
from the wood, gathering coppice poles, the figure
in my mind is not Gabriel Oak or Adam Bede
but Marie Antoinette dressed as a milkmaid in the
gardens of Versailles.

We prefer to suffer than to recover from those ills
that define us.

Life is our only frame of reference. Death brings an
end to everything, including itself.

How strange to be afraid of the dark. Even with the
lights on we have to go to sleep in our heads.

The gall, the presumption of that builder's shout:
"Cheer up mate, it might never happen." For all he
knows, it already has.

The atheist replacing God with human reason is
invoking something scarcely less elusive.

The pity of the world lies not in its horror but in the evolution of a mind capable of imagining that things might be otherwise.

Words sleep, dreamless as hills – until the eye reads either, line or land.

Love is the opposite of hate but friendship is its antidote.

The deepest pessimism is silent. Many a jeremiad against humanity is a vote of confidence in its prospects, as it presupposes a future reader to concur with its sentiments.

There may be mercy killings but there can be no mercy births.

Returning to the heath where I played as a boy, I found instead a desert of ash. In the hard world coming we will have to relearn many lost arts, including the art of losing.

"You make your own fate," say people born with the good fortune of never having had to prove it.

Love letter, love poem, love song... That a love aphorism is inconceivable ought to release us from the form for ever.

The aphorist: a fiction

Though we may become our obsessions, our obsessions rarely become us.

The aphorism is best suited to men who pronounce *ex cathedra* – it is the consolation of powerless erudition. Thus, to the world at large, he exists as a chartered surveyor; only in private does he attain on occasion the potency of memorable utterance.

Long ago, he used to wait for an aphorism to come to him. It would make its presence felt in a corner of his mind, like a mouse stirring behind the wainscot. To confront it too hastily was to risk its annihilation; so he learned to watch, as it were on the edge of his vision, the gradual resolution of the numinous entity until it was possible to determine not only its shape but also its content – as the wind reveals itself by the matter it plays with. Then, and only then, would he take up his pen and attempt to lure the words on to paper.

Latterly he has lost patience. Revealing a particular affinity for the abstruse, he forces himself to achieve the concision and pithiness which can only come of negligence.

A professional aphorist is a contradiction in terms. To sit down for six or eight hours each day, wilfully urging a precept into being, is to incur the wrath of the gods of definition.

Like most of his kind, he has a mania for concision. He dreams of nanotechnology capable of storing his observations *at a molecular level*.

The less sure he becomes of them, the more he relies on *italics* to give his writings a semblance of authority.

Perhaps she hopes that, by hiding his dictionaries, she might soften his resolve to aphorise. But there remain encyclopaedias, too substantial to impute their loss to accident, as well as radio, television, and the ever- expanding universe of the internet.

Each time she goes off on one of her rants, he sits there nodding while his mind retreats like a toad into its hollow.

His earlier manner used to be cool, insouciant. Now, seeing things clearly as never before, it is not unknown for him to declaim his aphorisms in the street. Curiously, the words seem to affect people less than the volume at which they are spoken.

Night, he replies when she wakes to find him writing, is far too precious to waste on sleep.

The aphorist is an autocrat on paper. He is deceived if he believes he can extend this authority into the domestic sphere.

Having watched her pack the last of her things, he returns to the frightening order of his study. Human love wanes, he writes; let love of maxims wax eternal.

Taken to task for non-attendance at work, he replies: "I can't be sacked for something I haven't done."

Food, he scrawls on supermarket produce, is only shit which is not yet up to scratch.

Drink, he murmurs, is the work of the cursing classes.

Paranoia, he might once have written, is masochistic megalomania.

At last, sensing that it is time for his oeuvre to be disseminated, he tears the manuscript into pieces and scatters them from the deck of the ferry.

Cremation is his last wish. He looks forward to the concision of ashes in an urn.

Though your feet be flat, you must stand on them.